Neighborhood Helpers

Jennifer B. Gillis

Rourke
Publishing LLC
Vero Beach, Florida 32964

www.rourkepublishing.com

PHOTO CREDITS: © Francis Twitty: cover; © Melissa Carroll: page 5; © Frances Twitty: page 6; © Yvonne Chamberlain: page 8; © Rick Rhay: page 9; © Jim Parkin: page 10; © Paolo Florendo: page 11; © Tomaz Levstek: page 15; © Roberta Osborne: page 17; © Rarpia: page 18; © Blaney Photo: page 19; © Sean Locke: page 20; © Talk Kienas: page 21; © Milan Radulovic: page 22

Editor: Robert Stengard-Olliges

Cover design by Nicola Stratford

Library of Congress Cataloging-in-Publication Data

Gillis, Jennifer Blizin, 1950-
  Neighborhood helpers / Jennifer B. Gillis.
     p. cm. -- (My neighborhood)
  ISBN 1-60044-203-X (hardcover)
  ISBN 1-59515-555-4 (softcover)
 1. Neighborhood--Juvenile literature. 2. Community life--Juvenile literature. 3. Occupations--Juvenile literature. 4. Professions--Juvenile literature. I. Title.
  HM761.G555 2007
  307.3'362--dc22

                                         2006022167

Printed in the USA

CG/CG

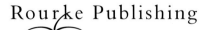

Rourke Publishing

www.rourkepublishing.com – sales@rourkepublishing.com
Post Office Box 3328, Vero Beach, FL 32964

Table of Contents

Neighborhood Helpers   4

Police Officer   6

Fire Fighter   8

Animal Control Officer   10

Mechanic   12

Librarian   14

Social Worker   16

Visiting Nurse   18

Doctor   20

Dentist   22

Glossary   23

Index   24

Neighborhood Helpers

The people in this book have jobs helping. They help in many ways.

Do you know some helpers like these?

Police Officer

Do you want to cross the street? A police officer can help you.

Police officers help people stay safe. There are police officers in your neighborhood.

Fire Fighter

Do you smell smoke? You can call the fire department.

Fire fighters put out fires. They keep people safe, too.

Animal Control Officer

Never touch an animal you find. Call an **animal control officer.**

Animal control officers help lost or hurt animals. They take them to **animal shelters**.

Mechanic

Is something wrong with your bicycle? A mechanic can help you.

Mechanics are helpers who fix things. There are mechanics for cars and bicycles.

Librarian

Are you looking for a book? A librarian can help you.

Librarians help people find **information**. They help people find books, too.

Social Worker

Do you have a problem at home or school? A **social worker** can help you.

Some social workers help children in school. Others visit people in their homes.

Visiting Nurse

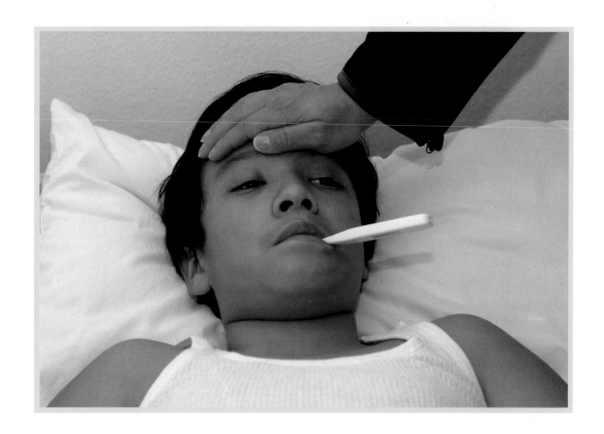

Is someone in your house sick? A visiting nurse can help.

Visiting nurses go to people's homes. They take care of people who cannot go outside.

Doctor

Did you hurt yourself? A doctor can help you.

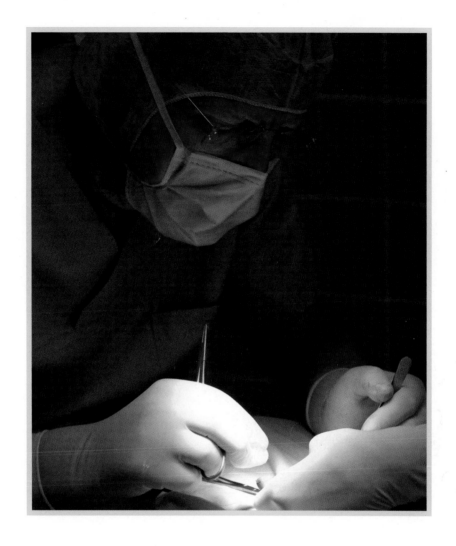

Doctors can put **stitches** in a deep cut. They can put a cast on a broken arm or leg.

Dentist

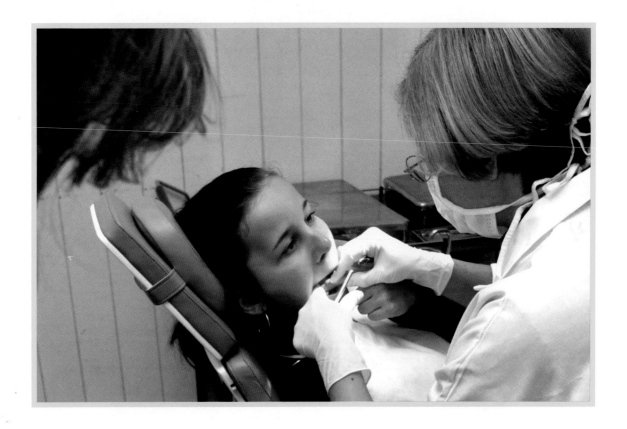

Do you have a toothache? A dentist can help you. Dentists can fix **cavities**. They can even pull a loose tooth!

GLOSSARY

animal control officer (AN uh muhl Kuhn TROL OF uh sur) — person who works for a town or county picking up loose or sick animals

animal shelter (AN uh muhl SHEL tur) — place where lost or sick animals stay until new homes can be found for them

cavity (KAV uh tee) — small hole in a tooth that can cause a toothache

information (in fur MAY shuhn) — facts people need to know

social worker (SOH shuhl WUR kur) —person who works for a school, town, or county helping people who have problems and making sure they get the things they need to solve those problems

stitch (STICH) — to close a cut by sewing with a special kind of needle and thread

INDEX

animals   10, 11

bicycle   12, 13

books   14, 15

fire   8, 9

home   16, 17, 19

people   4, 9, 19

problems   16

school   16

smoke   8

street   6

toothache   22

FURTHER READING

Ajmera, Maya. *Be My Neighbor*. Charlesbridge, 2004.

Caseley, Judity. *On the Town: A Community Adventure*. Greenwillow Books, 2002.

Rosa-Mendoza, Gladys. *Jobs Around My Neighborhood*. Me+Mi, 2002.

WEBSITES TO VISIT

www.sparky.org

www.americaslibrary.gov

www.mcgruff.org

ABOUT THE AUTHOR

Jennifer B. Gillis is an author and editor of nonfiction books and poetry for children. A graduate of Gilford College in North Carolina, she has taught foreign language and social studies in North Carolina, Virginia, and Illinois.